Psychic Awakening

Bernard
Ballard

These poems are to be read aloud.

ISBN: 978-09979008-0-4
Cover photograph by Christi Moon
Formatted by Cherry Shogren
Published by Bernard Ballard

Psychic Awakening

A key to the apprehension of the concepts presented in these works is an impossible idea, which supposedly occurred before the beginning of time. It goes like this:

From – "A Course in miracles"
Into eternity there crept a (tiny mad idea) at which the Son of God forgot to laugh. In his forgetfulness did the thought become a serious idea and possible of both accomplishment and real effects.

This idea is a perception of the mind, and is the cause of all the so called evil that exist. To correct this idea is to return to a way of being that is joy, peace, and abundance.

Perception.
All perception is a product of thinking. From thinking we "are" our minds, we begin to see that we have minds, and that it is the mind that has thoughts, beliefs, feelings and concepts.

There are many important questions that must be asked and answered in order to realize your truth. That is the purpose of these writing. You might call them myth, a dream, and illusion, a perceptual imagined reality based in relativity. It is all we have, here and now, to deal with, to uncover, and in so doing make life a joy instead of a drudgery

The mystic proclaims:

Our mind is our home in which we live and manifest this world.
As we clean up the microcosm in our mind then the macrocosm,
the world will clear up also.

Psychic Awakening

Table of content

Born to Have

I would be glad to come awake
if I thought that would make, or take
me to a place where dreams are real

me to a place where dreams don't kill

the truth of what I truly am
the truth of all that I could be
if I could open up and see
the things that I had dreamed before

the day I came into this place
of thought ideas torn apart

that you can see another part
of what it takes to make a world
of what it takes to make time curl
around and round, and not come round

to showing you an inch of truth

cause truth is not what shows up here.
It's just a place where I can play.

It is a space where I express.
It is a zone where only bone
ideas appear inside the light
of consciousness that is so bright

1

that it can turn straw into gold
that it can make the moon seem old
that it can take a sack of flour
and mold it into Eifel Towers

looking like they are a place
but truth be known, it is a waste
of time and space that causes us
to bend back down, to come around

like children learning how to ride
bicycles that will one-day fly
old cars that once were thought to die
new boats that help you to awake

from sleepwalking, that thing that makes

us believe we are what we're not
achieve the things that just do not
bring us true happiness and joy
or even give us time to toy

with powers we were born to have
with powers we forgot we have.
The power to bring peace, and love
to all we meet, to all the neat

places that we create in life.

This space where we've been taught to fight
to be the best of all that is,
Through all that is, is All that Is.

The first, and yes the last of you
provided you do not eschew
the idea there's only One.

The thought that your mind had become
so full of lies and true commands
that say it is your one demand
to believe that this world is real.

To believe that this world is thee.
The only place where time stands still.
It, it only exist as real
and true for those who're fast asleep.

They dream the dream of waking sleep.

They're all together, all as One
and rise in time to soon become
the thing that they have always been
that thing that's not a thing at all.

That thing that some folks even think
that they can tell the story. Be
in plays that show the truth in lies

in stories told, of I despise
and hate myself, what I've become
believing lies, I think I'm from
a place where we lay down and die.

A place where we all end up crying
for the things that only last
a year, or two, or even three
score years and ten, that come and go

so fast that it does make us old
believers in what we have made
beliefs that this, it only stays
in nightmare dreams that come when sleep's

forgotten and believed to be.

Called A Fold

The rainbow trout were of a clout
that I knew well before I fell
for all the lies were ever held

up high, for all of us denied
that we knew anything about
the kind of criminal that jails
were filled with in the days when we

escaped to find that we could see

much further, when we closed our eyes
in silence when we did decide
that seeing through the middle one
was wiser, for it brought forth fun

to know that All is well and good
for those who realized we could
continue in our ways of glad
and happy 'til even the sad

who told the olden tales again
around the fires at night, to wail
and mourn the things we felt we lost
to bye-gone modes of living life

which told of tales that only hold
attention for those golden toads

have fallen into ways of being
and seeing that could only be
the resurrected light from night
when sleep was used only for tools
to find the light that shined through all
that we perceived to be our foes.

Cause realizing it takes two
to fight and die, or live and kill
ideas that don't work no more
ideas that were held back for

to keep us in the kitchen sealed
with sinks, were filled up to the brim.

Without ideas, we did start
as children when we all could fart
without the shame and blaming of
another who might live to come

back into innocence and know
that this is why we're called a fold.

We all are born with knowing things
that transcend all that is the way
of practiced thought, down here on earth
when we are taught pure lies to start

our journey back into the start
of letting go of things are taught

by those who only follow form
instead of trying to re-mourn
the ways that never change a thing
except our minds believing lines

that died out centuries ago
and hide the truth that can't be known

by folk, to take the oath to go
not into fields where freedom dwells.
It's far more easy, to get to hell.

Decide Alone Inside

It's finally time to write again.
To sit upright, and take my pen
while sweat, it seeps out from my veins
and covers me as if some sane

republican had chose to go
about the old ways that dispose
of anger held for all the rest.

Those democratic fools that best

the idea that we can deal
with troubles made that seem for real
to all the folk who stand today
in folds that will not go a way

that's guided by the ones who say
as guided by the fellows say.

You can do anything you want.
For time will tell the true about

whatever you decide to do
in life always comes back on you
to show and prove what you did say
is right or wrong, which is to say.

What you decide is right and true
turns out to be the same as you
decide alone, inside your mind
though you may feel that all they say

ought have no bearing, not take caring
what those fools and folks do say
that folks been schooled to do and say
what's written in the books of old

where understanding is encoded
deep beneath the surface meaning
on those scrolls which are so bold
to tell you that you are the way

was lost in seas that seem a way
that never could be true at all
for everything that changes will
be never more, remembered well.

Yet all that, fore, ever tells
the true about which way to go

as Love, and Peace, and Joy can never
go away unless you grow.

To seek in silent stillness where
your mind does need no time at all
to know the true, to be as well
as angels are the higher thoughts

that never learn to tell a lie
or make a choice or decide I
may take the longer road around
to teach myself a way that's not.

The way all fools, they choose to go
to see what they might find and know
if water is as good as wine

9

if lying is the way to find
if killing beats the way that we
do know, could never be of He
who is as one, the only One

from which all truth and light supposed
do imitate from out of none
that does exist in time and space
but does project it's thoughts about

a place that don't exist at all
except in minds that took the fall
into that separation place
to play duality a while

until the mind does realize
that playing in these form built ways
can never take you out of place
except to finally realize

that all things are the way they are
cause you decide, cause you behold
these separation thoughts that fold
you into dual thoughts that seem

the opposite of what is true
for those who see through middle eyes
that cannot close, that are not blind
by light filled shadows which define

the world of form that you've designed
with thoughts of separation's ways
to have a place to play and stay

until you waken and are saved

from lies that can't be seen in light.

Doing the Things

Doing the things you're suppose to
the things that you are not

is the only way to know.
Ooh yes, the only way to go
if you wish happiness to come.

If you wish happiness to bum
you out of time, you out of rhymes

which tell the truth, which brings back youth

to all your senses made to be
the way you tell, the way you smell
your way to life, and love and peace.

The that, that you came here to be
the things that you came here to see.
To play it out, to make it real

is the One thing that you have killed.
The only thing that you do feel.
The only real thing, makes you kneel

to all the lies and doubts that peel
away the truth, the way to go
if you do truly want to know
the way to go, the way to know

what's right and good enough to try
the things are good enough to keep
on doing now, on doing for
the life of me that knows the truth.

The only way that you can find
once you've gone other's ways and know
that this is not, that this can't be
the truth of life I want to know.

The truth of death, that isn't so.

The real and good, it looks like gold.
It smells like children when they wake
up from a sleep that is so deep.
So deep and wide that it does keep

them in a rhyme that will not peep
in on the true way that's to go
on that, the only way to know
is give it all you've got to give

is live your life, and it will give
you choices, show which ways to go.
Your choices, show which way brings gold.

The gold of knowing for yourself
what's not the treasure that's lived for
and then again forgot.

To believe things that bring nightmares.
You do the things that you would swear
would give you ways to hate, thus bake
up stories told, not made of gold

but stories you find out are hell
are hellish things that you now swear
will never do again, or dare.

But how could you, you ever find
the truth of life without the
so called
sin that brought the doubt.

The things you did that showed without
a tinge of goodwill, that's about
the only way to know without
a doubt that you made a mischance.

The only way to know your choice
for life, and love, was the wrong phrase.

A phrase that brought you to a place
where you can see, want to erase
the things you've done, allowed to come
into your life, the thing you wished

you could undo the things that show
you were a fool, but fools find out
in time. In time they know again
that this is not the way to go

if you would will, be out of code.
If you would will, find the real goal.

The goal that life, and love, and peace
will only be, will only come
to you once you have played the bum

are things that cannot come to you
until you've made the choice to do
what's wise to do, what's truly you

have found out, you ought not to do
the roads mom says you ought not take
are roads that show a better way.

It must be found. It must be made.
For ways I've tried have failed to bring
me hay the ways I've tried, have brought
delays to everything I dream

would make me take

the happiness that I deserve
the joy, the gift can only lift
me up if I have done, denied
the truth of lies that I've despised.

that never last?

For life is up, and life is down.
At least it seems to be in time.
At least it seems to make these rhymes
that show me why I'm here today.

This place I've made without delay.

Ego Gone A Way

My freedom born of desperation
taking on initiation

to the way I ought, to be
imagined in all that I see
that comes in dreams that say I can
illumine all, the this, I am

a nation born to idle thought
that gains control as if I bought
a crock of shit, from books and schools
that teach me things that I tell you

can never be expressed for less
then glory days that do impress
my ego, gone away to sail
and free me from those thoughtful tales

that I can't take inside to find.

They all are lies that have defined
my separated self become

the image of what I did sum
to be the true of who I claim
to be in fantasies I planned

to show myself what I am not
and then, thus to begin to fuss
and fight the images I've made
to counteract being the slave

of loving All that Is, will be
of giving all that I can see.

Forgiving all I thought was wrong
and being just what I've become
in present moment, here, I am

the One who can't seem to pretend.

It all is just a game of chance
that is made up to give romance
a chance to stand still, and be still.

Just do your best and know you're healed

whenever you surrender stances
made to give yourself the chance
to waken. Form this dream, and win

the knowledge that you're All there Is

experiencing life in form
to gain the mountain top again.
To know that you're the only One.
Cause one times one times one is One.

Ego Must

I've finally found the answer too

The question I've been asking you
about the time, about the space
ideas that had formed this race

to get a way, to get today
to be, outside the truth, that Is

to be some way that is not here
but presupposed, yet re-exposed
to be whatever it is not
because we say and do believe.

There is a better or a worse.

That their way is a higher one
or just to have ability
to know and see that it is me
who thinks his is the only way

to get in time, to re-define
what ought, or should, or would be well

enough to give you life, as well
as all this world might show and tell
the reasons I believe I'm right

is cause my ego must be shown.
Because the ego must be known
and glorified and testified
to be the righteous way to go.

To please those people who control
opinions that we all do know
must be appeased, must be received

to matter on this walk of life

where no one cares, where everywhere
is seen to be what no one dare
be satisfied to be the real

and true and only way to be

content to say, and see, and be
this moment here. The One that's now
and ever, only what can be
outside of time and outside space.

It is the only, can erase
ideas formed inside your mind
to change what is, to what should be
or ought to not, or maybe should

be what is happening today.
This moment now.

The only time can be outside of pace.

Forgetfulness To Help

The images that you do view
in life they all do come to you
to show you things that you do gain
once you believe, and take the steps

to see them manifest in your
imagination as it swells
itself in ways that cannot be
unless you truly want to see

or if it's fear in this career
that you give time and token to.
Those thoughts will also come to call
in your experience of life.

That is the reason we do use
forgetfulness to help you do
the things that you did fear before

are gone away, that can no more

be trouble in the future day
that you imagine from the past
that participle that does cast

it's light to show what can't be true

but giving time in places feared
but spending time in thoughts about
in worry, doubt, it all is that

the energy that you have backed

your stories with that make the fact
to all appearing in your dream
of, I can't do, or I can't see
myself appearing that, that tree

or storm that drives you into there.
Where you must go to shed the lies
that come about, that were forgot
to keep you in this, placed to dare

to be or see what you are not
and make it so that you forgot.
There's nothing that you cannot do
or be, or have that is not thee.

Unless your dreams are taken for
the true of you, the truth to be

once settled in your mind will find
a way to get you back in time
to go along with all the rest
to come to be a place of rest

where you can be your own true Self
imagining the days are best
when followed down the way without
those doubts and all your fears left out

side, after rain turns into sun
and you do find that you have run
around and round and finally come
back here to where you started from.

I Am Telling You

What can I do, where can I go
to stop this wholly, holy feeling

I get when burning, with distress.
Time when I have, and yet am not
the fellow that I used to be.

The One that I was taught is me
who sits in silence everyday

who will not let it be dismay
but joy, above the things that kill
the truth that life is what we be

that life in truth, is all that we
or anyone has to become

aware and know it's no mistake
to close your eyes and to awake
from dreaming dreams that make it seem

like we are here in form that falls

asleep in every single day
of living life within this day
outline that some believe defines
the truth of who, and what, and why.

But bodies don't think anything
but bodies only do the things
the mind commands, it makes demands.
The body only follows hands

that guide it, this way or to that
where it is shown and told to go
by thinking, feeling, living minds
that think that they can re-define

the truth of who, and when, and where
we follow going down the stair.
We follow round, and round, and bound
to see it's me who is so blind

to think that bodies, they can sin.

To think that God could call, to pin
us up like fools who cannot tell
the true from lies I'm telling you

that minds were made to live inside

these fellowships that do define
what I believe, I never knew
and what I know cannot be new.

For it Is, and has always been
inside the Field, that's truly me
inside the Zero Point of Light.
Besides, you know that we are bright

enough to know the truth of life.
When we are still enough to kill
these thinking little minds that spill
out false beliefs that almost kill

the truth that we all knew before
we found our way to re-display
the olden ways of playing dice
with feeble thinking that won't last.

Until in time, when time stands still
we realize that we can't kill
cause life is life, and cannot die.

What folly fools believe these lies

made up in fairies tales that sell
you out of knowing Now, can smell
the true way, Cause, It's only known

by those who step there, I suppose

and place their trust in selfless being
the way that we were made to be
the way that we can always see.

The way that God created thee

to be the perfect image made
of light, and love, and peace and joy.
Not separations, that's supposed!
Not fallen pieces that can't see

that it's all just a dream come true.

A dream that you imagine you
can be, and see to find it out.
To know yourself, and then at last

to know you are the Son of Source
that you are All, and yet are part
extending from the place outside
of time and space where silence is

to be you, still, and close your eyes.

Be silent and you only find
what revelates and vibrates too
to manifest the island dress
that you've put on to stand in time.

Enough to see, and tell your lies
until you open up that eye
that can't be seen and cannot lie.

For it's the portal place where saints
and saviors come to E-erase
the lie that life can become death
when all we know has come to rest

on hope, and dreams of future time
on believing that the Divine
needs time or space, to make in haste
these things that only eat and taste

the surface of what's real and true.
This place that I am telling you
that moves, and shakes, and seems to die.

It only changes form to spy

out all that life has here to sell
to fools who want and cannot tell
that they are all, the All that Is
appearing here to feel the thrill

of doing that which can't be done
in place, in time that stands so still
that it is all potential 'til
someone awakes, and life begins

again.

Ideas You Pretend

I'm stuck inside this life I feel.

So full of rage that I appeal
to anything or any One
to come into this place and be

a reason that I want to see

why I can't find that part of me
that does support this fool upstart
who thinks he knows the way to go

and really why it seems to be

the only thing was re-conceived
to fill me full of fear and doubt
about the reason I've come out

of satisfied relief, to pout
about this life that I pretend.

I'm satisfied that I have lived
for long enough to give the give
and take the take of all who have
not lost their way, but only stay

inside this Rose of graves exposed.
That tell these tales that do suppose
to show me what is right and wrong
with all I've thought and been in time.

That I, might finally define

the reasons I have come to go
the final life that has survived
both all the things I've thought about
and all the things I've been, to bout

this life esteemed to be what is
the only thing that Christ esteemed

about the living and the dead

both memories about, instead
of letting go, well, once again
these ideas that you pretend
are real and true, and all of you

have fallen for, that which seems
so nice
that you need never be the spice
left out of all your ways of being

and seeing just how masterful
the game of dice can play your life.

As if it's all that's natural
to live and die, and then to cry
instead of accepting the cost
of being boss, of being lost

is that you have finally found
the only way back home

is to forget, and then remember
ways and means that only you
and I can play these memories

until they all do fall away.

Jest or Test

Test your true ability
and see if life will not show thee
the way to know, the way to stay
the things that have been getting way

from all of your ability
to see, and say, and not delay
the truth that I am telling you
the truth that one day will make free

all of those others said to be
the One that went, and thus did see
the things that take you round and round
the things that finally let you down

to the, that place of dreams come true.

The earth, that place that will show you
the thing that you were led to be.

Things believed, thus do show thee.

What you are not, what you can't be
in places born beyond the sea.

Of I can't do a thing I want
of things desired out of the Be.

Beginnings, where I once told thee
to not delay, or you will see
the thing that dogs and cats can see
the things that don't make sense to see

that all your lies believed came true.

So say the truth and you will see
that anything is possible.
That all the things you think can be

developed into holograms
that show you scenes you will believe

about the power of words can tell
that smell and taste, do bring dismay
to your true sense, of knowing me.
To your reality you see

that Gods on high who play these games
that Gods deny that things can be
the opposite of truth, is lies.

The lies espied when you denied
that you could become what's not so
that you might be the One who sees

the thing become, and run, and hide.

The things that I am telling you
escape your knowing, and appear
inside this dream landscape you fear

to realize it's all made up.

A place to show just what you may
create these things I'm telling you
that no one else can see, or do
to show yourself to be the king.

The magic deemed, before your knees
were bent to know you can stand up
upon the hill and be for real.

That creations the oldest game
invented by those crafty things
who don't know what to say or do.
Who did not want to tell you to

be still and know that I AM God..

You won't believe it 'til you see
what you have done and thus become
the God on Mount Olympus hill.
The Ones who really made the kill.

The Ones who did it for the thrill
of seeing what they say and see
of trying out these new born skills
of finding how to cast the dice

and then forgetting out of spite
that fools find out, they have delayed
the truth of knowing what is free.

For those born out of knowing not
from those in thinking I cannot
take all the blame, assume the shame
of life and death built in the games

of going down beneath the mist
of running through this lengthy maze
of forgetting why you are here
of knowing why, and when, the way.

Too, to get up off of your knees

and knowing you're the Son of God
as all the others, all around
who play these games without delay

of knowing not, quite where to stay

in safety where your Father lives
in safety where your Mother gives
instruction to this Child gone wild.

Instructions to the One will find
his way back out, from in the mist.
His way out of the foggy bliss
that takes you to that place called hell.

The play where all the minions dwell
that forgot why they have come here.
Who don't know why they're staying here
in place, in space, in time to find

that everything here is divined
to show you ways to learn about
the opposite that can't be found
until you've fallen into mist.

Unless you miss that flavored kiss
of Love, and Light, and Peace today.
The only way to make your hay
is to be still, and smell the air

that can't be seen, or heard, or found
in sights, and sound that come around
in sights that always do confound
the true beliefs that you conceived

33

before the split that cannot be

cause all things are contained in One
cause all things are become from One.
The One that we believed fell down
but only bent him down to find

a new and different way to be
outside the dream of I can be

the good, without the bad denied.

That it is bad, it just plain hides
the fact that it is just and act
to show you that you made all that

to play the game, to know what's shame
and doubt, and fear, they all confine
you to that place called hell and death.

Those things can't be unless you jest
about the truth of life that's One.

It comes around and thus will find
that all the things you say and do
will come about, will come to you.

So why not believe you can do?

Be. Be the things that will save you
from all confusion, and your will
will save the day, and live your thrills.

The thrills that show you God can do
all of the things I'm telling you
that you must leave your fears and doubts.
Yes, you must leave your I cannots.

You. You come, come yourself and know.
You are the ONE.

Know Not Who

The Oboe sung before it had come
to celebrate the time gone by
in time where I cannot connive

the things that are baked off the day
I separated from the rest.

The ones who thought that it was jest
to celebrate, to bring our calls
into a place of faith, and waste
our thought that brought us here before

we were the Ones who used to bore
our way into the way of kings.
Those beings who would not conceive
or bear the boring things that sin.

The Song of God knows why we die
to songs that know not how to die
of place in space where it does taste
of license I forgot I had

of dividends that made me glad
to be the first born of a race
that could not see, much less believe
that we could fall, or keep us down

that we would keep going around
that we could ever have forgot
the things that we are made to see
and be it all before we knew

the ways that keyed us from our knees
to stand up tall and never fall
again for lies that all do drive
us into pain to make us gain

a way of seeing what is real
a way of seeing without frills
the gain we got and then forgot
to share with all our kin and friends.

The Ones who went a different way
discovered rules, and drank the booze
that made them see in ways that we

could not come to before the fall
of all those ideas befall

us all, in time and space erases
truth from lies, and lies decide
who we must be, what we conceived
in valleys filled with raven blood

in sordid places where we waste
out time, with schemes that can't achieve
the way of bees, the ways that we
first put on when we first arrived

first put on, back before we were
the object of so much that saved
us from becoming, numbers running
people know not how, or why

or when, or who it is that used
to be in sight, and be in sayings

that one day, all were written down
that one day all were burned to hell
to help us to develop ways
that were before the books were nailed
into our minds that had forgot

that we don't need no others thoughts
that we don't need no time at all
that we are One and cannot fall
for tricks that last a thousand years

for treats that keep us in the fear
of things that don't exist at all
of all those things I made us fear
that we could ever not get back

to being true, to knowing you
and I, that we are just the same
in Light and Love, and not to shame

or blame, or doubt it's all a dream

in which confusion is the theme
where anything believed becomes
where all things have become, come from
a mind that cannot know the truth.

For it is still and silence, still.
We'll know it all when we awake
to drift free in the stream, the One
who came up from the mist.

That One who did refuse the kiss
of Mother Nature's born to run
around, and round and thus become
the way that shows us truth from lies.

The things that no one can despise
as long as they refuse to come
up out, and then to re-become
the opposite of lies, is truth.

The only way to reconnect
to what we have come here to do
and see the reasons that we be
and live in houses made of stone

that will not float, or fly, or dive
into those spaces far from places
dreamed in dreams that cannot be
awareness full, and real, and thrilled

to finding bliss, the way to kiss
beyond below, and to thus know
that we were made to be the king
of our desires making me, the One.

The One who can remember all
before the fallen one appeared
to be what he was not endeared.

These frosted cakes that can't be baked

or heated up, or taken down
because there is no way around
the truth that now appears.

Love That Lacks

The three things show you are divine
come not from living with the swine
or elephants that we call blessed

or normal folk who seem to rest
on all the rules and all the goals

that have been set by those who know
a way or two that worked before

to prove themselves to be much more
then anyone who's come before
into this circle where we swirl
around and round like bells in tow

that sound there chimes out to the world
that doesn't take no thought at all
about the lack or all that backs
the idea we can't be One.

For look around, you'll see you're from
a place where all men seem to race
around to gain and hold the gate

so no One, who is filled with blame
and shame can ever enter in
to get a drink, to quench his thirst
to look into the mirror worse

to see if he might visualize
a time when he did not decide
to not depend on what is seen
or heard or talked about in church.

For Christ, he seldom went in there
where serpents always seem to dare
to go and take off all the views
exchanged to show they're not like you

not ordinary folk who walk
the streets and never seem to talk
as if they know the way back home
might be envisioned in a dream

might come awake, and yet not seem
to be the true, or yet the right.

For never in those books held high
could I remember seeing why
or how, or when, or where we came
into ideas, we are fare

and care enough to let life go
and be the sea of saying we
declare inside to be the truth
accepted by our own true bliss

while living lives that seem to be
the opposite of what's told me
by all those folk who read the books
in Sunday schools, and schools that tool

your belief to remain the same
and all those folk who do seem lame
enough to follow all those rules

41

and yet they never smile, or lose
their judgment on their fellow man.

The Ones who say that, they can't stand
inside the box of I cannots
or I refuse to listen to
what's read and taught in black and white.

It's all so filled with love that lacks
ability that we're all in
the boathouse that has left the laws.

Of Newton's laws and civil crimes

dictated by the Ones who claim
that they're the only ones God loves
and all the rest must go by dales
where fruit and famine are the cost.

To understand that black and white
are two terms used to sell you on
the lack of facts that you could use
to show yourself there is no lack.

It's you desiring what's in back
of tales that speak of future years

when dead men will arise with tears
to find their life is just begun
again to see just how the One
can never die, but leaves this place

of time and space to solve the case
that no one who won't close their eyes
and be, and see within the lies
that judgment places on us all

and then appears to re-become

to manifested destiny

that we wish on the other Thees
who rode around all over town
but failed to stop their mind to find

that dreams are not the only time

or rhyme that tells the tales that we
believe when we are fast asleep
in nightmare robes that cross the globe

denying this is all that Is

or was, or will be in these dreams
of separation, made to crest
and fall apart to make you rest
these false ideas thought about

and made so real that all of us
except the One, who sits real still
in innocence, can stand the chill
of living in the place in space

where time stands still and all is well.

That spot that has no form at all
or way of being can be told
or judged, or thought about for naught
outside the vine can be made into wine.

That truth that we are all, outside of form
divine.

Placed On Parade

The way we fall apart, shows when
we need some help to claim the bank
of vision's quest, that I have had

to make me tired, to make me mad
enough to believe all the lies
that I have found out by and by

by trying out the forms of life
that I have given to be mine
in mind, made dreams that always seem

to be what's real, and true to those
who lost the tool that any fool
may follow, to the Amore way.

To see again what they might say
once they have taste, and touched, and felt
a different key to know if we'd

decide this is the route to take
to make it home, or to get grown.

So used to living with these lies
that seemed to free me, yet disguised
the awesome fear that had appeared
wherever I believed I died

and realized on waking up

that all the tales I've told today
about a day when skies will fall
are just those fairies tales believed

when we are young and did believe
whatever children can expose
to young and old who know the code.

The quantum code that carries all

our DNA and causes way
too much to grow a way, from old
ideas that taught a God could fail

and man could not come to be known
to follow too, the way that you
have come to be, to show that She
the Spirit side might make the claim

not offer blame

but just decide that it is lame
to give the reason in a season

toned down, by the reasons why.

Those distant tales about old whales
or fish in dreams, that seem to gleam
with words of truth found out in youth

to be the way some Gods communicate.

To show the lost, who left the path
the One, unmarked by trail or map.
The One you'd chosen for your self

to follow too, to see if you
were truly free and well.

For what is Love if it don't free.

It's filled with fear to know that you
are free but have achieved a state
of mind called fantasy to think.

That anything God makes is like

to say a program tells its maker

well, which way to go

which way it goes

against the programming it can
not make mistakes, not change the make
not set a date that can't be known
that can be grown out of its own
capacity.

So if its grace you say that makes
a One so free, a One like me

who took the gift, who made the cliff
to stand so high out in the Light
and know that none of this is right

but just a way placed on parade
to show just how, when, where and why
a One can choose. Go any way.

47

That Living Soil

I'm in a state of blissful joy.
I don't know why or what it's for.

But as I waken from this dream
it seems I have the high esteem

it takes to notice, all is well
as good, to know I need not go
and do, or tell, or sell a thing
to get what makes most men insane.

Believing they have lack and loss
they spend their lives in games that toss
a way all things that bring you joy
away all that they could employ

to gain that peace that gives you joy
enough to know that living soil

is not a thing that God would make.

It's just reflection that does take
the image of what can't be told
or taught
or shown by those who know
that spirit beings have no form
that children of the Sun don't run.

They have no place to go or come
but just imagine inside minds
that have forgotten that the key
lies hidden inside bells believed

to be the sounding stones that grow
inside of things that I don't know

but made up, out of lies defined
to be a place to realize
our thoughts, and feelings which have made
this world of opposites to tame

our false beliefs which manifest

in form, like beings that display
the opposite of what is real
the polarized divided signs
that represent what cannot be

except in movies that we see
are like a staged display of times
in reels that show what the divine
might do if it were separate.

But motion pictures never get
to be the true, or not the lie
which all the fools declare to be
the only thing that they can see

and thus believe that it is me
and you, and they, that live this lie
of false hopes built up on a line
where everything is born to die

49

and dying makes you realize
that surface things can separate

in dream like states that don't awake
to truths that only mountain men
can know and be, until they land
again back where they have come from

in blissful states where all is One.

Not form, or fancy states of mind.

No colors seen, that do not blend
to be known here, and be seen now
where time stands still, and does allow
us all to waken from this dream.

The One Who Dreams

Now here I AM, and there you are
a sitting here upon the bar
deciding what it is I'll make

in life experience, will take

me to that place in time and space
to see again, what I might choose
a different way to go before.

This life in form comes to transform

that, that is not, into what Is.
The true, the real, the I do form
myself into the things I'm not
to show myself that I can be

and do all things because I'm free.

I'm made in image just to be
and see, and say all things that we
decide to have experience
to show, and tell that I am more

than we could ever hope to be
in life times that only show me
that life on earth's a place to rest
from being all, and knowing best

ways to amount to nothing less
then all that Is, might call it blessed
to step into these earth suits, see
if I can remember it's me

and he, and she also play these

parts

of I can't do a thing apart
from this, my true reality

is quantum, formless, yet performs
in space and time to make these rhymes

in order to provide in time
and space, a place to re-erase
ideas that turned out so base
that you can't tell the true from false

until you step out of your nest
of feeling safe, and well, and good.

To try out life on earth, you should
do all the things that make you doubt
be all the other ways that sprout
out life that has been taught is lost

might be the only way to find
what's real, what's there, inside this land

created to allow your plan
of separation to be read
and seen for what it truly is
beyond all doubt and hopelessness.

You find you always raise the case
to be the One who fell asleep
and dreams these dreams in sleep to see
the things in mind that he believes.

He is in form, and fancy ways
that may delay, but cannot stay.

A part of Life. For it's for real
and never ever could it kill
the everlasting and eternal
part of you that's whole and well

and always tells the truth to be
that you, and I will always be

the One who dreams

these dreams to see what he is not
but finally awakens too
the truth within, whenever he
begins again with silent stillness

frees the mind

from being bound in space and time
from thinking separation thoughts
from playing in this pond called earth.

Throw Into the Ganges

My house, my life, my love and peace.
The sheets inside my bed so neat.

All that I have to give and share.
All of those things that I do swear
were given me to give me life

that I forgave, and brought me back
into this life that I've survived

into this way that some despise.
It is an image, just a privilege
wrapped inside of wineskins dined

to re-divide the infinite time

that always lets you, to reside
in ways that show you who you are
in wild displays that show you hell

or heaven is no place at all

but just a state you can recall

when you are still, when you feel well
enough to be, and do and dare
the things that you are right to know
and be, and see and image He

or She who only feels the light

as insight that comes out so bright
that shows you this is all a dream.
A seam in time that some believe
can never come or go in time.

Allow them now to re-define
the way that others must behave
to be accepted in their way
of knowing what is said and told

by all those others I suppose
who feel this life is all that is.

It's so important to just live

to gain all that you can, and then
to realize it's all for naught.
For one day we must all return
to spirit beings who deserve

that we don't need nothing at all.
That we are all, if you recall
that Christ and Buddha came awake.
They needed nothing to mistake

these bowls of food that we decide
the only way to see and find.

Truth With Lies

I don't know what to say, or what to do
about this field inside of you

and outside of, and up above
the sights and sounds that I do know
are all a part of who I am

no more than blue belongs to me
or you, or they who read this tale
that I suppose is in a way
the story told from inside out

of what I think and what I'm taught
to feel and claim as both my own

but I don't know, and I don't show

the way around that others say
and do obey, so they may stay
inside the box of I don't know
a thing except what I am told

but deep down inside of my being
there lies a Light that always knows

and only recalls what the spies
did tell, in tales about the whys
that do detail, and reveal truths
were hidden to all those would spoil

the righteous way which is to go
the next small step, and know it's best

to follow to, and for this side
that raises out of all the lies
that are espied once you decide
to tell the tale that is beside

the mystery that can't be known
about these tales, and all the whys
that I decide to realize
by sitting still, and by and bye

I know not why, but I do I
become the things that lead a way
that can't be told to those who go
a way that's not what most would say

is fast becoming, that which is they
who bind themselves to ideas taught
to be the way to live at life
instead of being, just what does

sing, inside the mind that isn't mine

yet knows me well, as you could tell
if you believe what can't be known
or shown to those who believe lies
about a place in time, where I reside

in dreams that show just what I've known
to be the teleed-vision that I share

with all those others gone to sleep

and waking to what can't be seen
or told, or talked about to fools
who follow rules and only go
the way that they are told to live

and give of things that can be seen
and touched in ways, don't prove a thing
except what I thought I might pray
in words and phrases turned about

the way that my perception, perceives doubt

or faith in traveling the road
that I have chosen well, to go
to see if I can be my Self.

The part that has no doubts
has always let
It to my intuition stayed
in present moment where I weight

the truth, with lies that can't be true
to any but the Ones who chose
from waking state, that always knows
and goes the way that they divine.

Vibrations Are the Way

The ancient One came down again
to settle into time, again
he came even through time remained
to all who did remain.

Besides there was yet space again
to place inside all of the things
that never were, or ere could be
the way they told the tales

of how we all decided to
come over to the side that you
had chosen to, decided was
the way made most of our desires

to live inside these homes that were
out in the rain, so filled with pain
that all our centers were again

the space in time, was placed in place
to help us find our way.

'til once again, the clouds they opened
up to allow us our frightened
ways and means to break away
and see what we had done

to become all that was in time.
All that which did remain in space
without having to re-erase
the way that it had been before

there was a space in place to live.

Our lives, we first divided with
decisions made to hasten all
our faculties and place us in
these realms where all have come

to meditate and take us from
the ideas that life was built..

The reasoning that caused our fall
to places where it all could call
this life on earth, that we should know
what we are not and could not be

forever and a day.

Now, allow me to re-explain.
They only were for us to gain
our senses back, was to attach
those lies by staying still.

Allowing them. Come back and back
and making it a false attach
upon themselves, their own true lies

because they truly dis, despised
the way that they had chosen to
make up these stories told

of living death, where there's no rest
from being lost in senseless gross
and ignorance was what could see
and be seen all around.

Both you and I, we both wore frowns
as we did pace, and come around
a second time and then a third
until we finally heard the word

come out of us, the final word
that we call Namaste.

Then all the crowd did gather round
to look up high, and all were bound
to know the true way is to go.
To go nowhere at all

but simply open up our ears
to just be still, and know it's here.
Remain in ways that one might call
us all together once again

to know without having to tame.
To feel it all within our field.
To re-apply all but the lies.
To form a brand new way.

For we have always been the One
in days of old, the ancient One
who had forgot to stay his tongue
had put him in this place

where sound vibrations were the way
to begin all the things we may
have thought, or dreamed until it seemed

the proper thing to do and be

to find that we are all the One
remembering in days that come
around and round 'til all fall down.

Then all get up to show instead

a different way to play it out.
This life that will always remount
to play the scout, 'til time runs out

again.

It's all to show and tell my friend.
A game of chance, romance my friend
where Love's the golden key, my main

to being well and true

to living life as if romance
is not a game called dice my friend
'til all might take a chance, and then
be shown you cannot lose.

For all come from the same old place.
That space where time and space erase
the idea of truly knowing
all you are, and all you've been

and all you'll be again.

Inside this dream where all who run
the course that has been set, and come
to fullness and thus does erase
the lies that we accept with haste

to get ahead, to show that death
can never come to be.

Ways Called Sin

I do think, that I could take
myself into a better place

then knowing everything's all right
and good, until you make the choice
to separate, and thus to bless
ideas which claim it is best

to follow, on your way to hone
those talents that do all belong

to One, who takes the time to bide
in patients, which is all you need
to scale that mountain made from sin.

That Idea, you used to win
the battle back into the grave.
For no one here ever escapes

that trials, that are all a part
of getting well, of going far
enough into those ways called sin

to discover that it is in
these challenges, that you were bred
to overcome these lies that spread

about a God who makes you go
and do the things that you behold
in order to find out what's right
and what can never bring delight

but demonstrates what does not work

which shows and tells the means that will
lead you down roads that might appeal
a little better if you chill

your judgment, that calls it a sin

when you are human and begin
to follow out these whims called sin

which are your curiosity defined

to be a thing that's not allowed
by those, who say you should not go
a way may lead too, to your death

but truth be told, you cannot know

until like Prodigal, you do go
and try it out so you can see

the true reason that you achieve
a higher way of knowing truth
that cannot be found here on earth
where everything appears, to have

an opposite to make it sound

advice that I am telling you.
Some things, you just cannot be found
until you take the time to climb
up high above and down below

to see what it is you behold
by trying out yourself to know
if it is good or is fool's gold.

So why deny yourself the try
to prove it good or find it's not
because it's written, that will cook

you up in hell instead of tell
and show you what is right and good
to take it up or let it go.

Whatever's Written Down

The whistle blew again and then
I knew if I wrote down again
a note or two, before I knew

I'd waken fully from my sleep.

I opened up my eye to see
if I might spy out truth again
that was so hidden when with sin

that error, thought, was born to win

your senses over to the kin
who fellowship to gather in
the motive way, begun with them

to strengthen up their doubts and fears

to know whatever's written down.
It must be true. It can be found
to be the thing the others say

can't be a lie, can't be denied

for who would take the time to grow
in ways that always felt this cold
like waves of winter breezes freezes
truth into the pillars salted

by refusals to take forward
steps, and not look back to lack.

That had become the greatest dear
of all those were, so filled with fear
that tales told of the olden days
might come again and settle in

to lives, were so afraid to live
in present moment and begin

to create a new way to be
and see, and say that was not known
to fools who never take the chance
to try out things not written down

and followed by those others from
the proven task, they say must last
until the final day arrives
when God returns to take us home.

Yet wasn't that two thousand days
or was it years when he said from
his mouth that he would soon return

that he might take us all to task
to do the things that he said last
forever and a day, a night
when we might realize at last.

We cannot be the devil's child.

For we are born into this night
to satisfy our own true love
of finding light in our own time.

But time is made by minds designed
to follow sun, and moon, and stars
instead of realizing that.

We are that light.

Who Knows Best

I'm swept all over and am back
to living life as if the back

of carts, that carry all our gear
the stuff we have when we are here
to stay the cause, to just do all
we can to make it through the night

that becomes all who make the try
at living life in freedom now.

The only time that ever thrives.
The only time that is for real.

The only place in time and space
not future, or stores out of past
creations that you made, that you
might share with all the folk around

who wander in the world of fools
who don't know who they are or why.

They reinvested all their time
in climbing up this ball of slime
that seems to be for real, as real
as feathers on a donkey's back.

Why do we waste our time in cheer
of things that never last too long
of things that never could belong
up on the list of things I need

like all the opposites I've faked
to give me more time to erase
the idea I AM born free
but set immediately to see

and find and learn the things that bring
me into this capacity

where all I do or say, or see
is regulated by the ones
that I look to, and believe in.

Cause all my family and friends
know more and better than I can
trust my own instincts and believe

that just below, my way of being

is still, the Lightest that God brings
me back into my own true Love.

That won't release me, or let go
but waits in willing confidence
until I'm tired of being thrilled
by all the things, that make no sense

to One who believes he knows best.

What he should do, or she should not
in just the things that give, or got
us here, into this ball of twine

a looking for the kind of plan
to save our self, and save the world
from madness that does seem to swirl
around in all the minds that bind

together to make life on earth.

Our greatest challenge, left to be

ourselves, and see how silent we
can make our mind, and thus divine
the best way we can live again.

EKPHRASTIC POETRY
(Wisdom Writings)

Poems in Rhyme and Riddle
Unravel the Riddle
The Unsolvable Riddle

(meditations for awakening)

What is the question answered in this poetic
riddle?
Formulate four questions that must be asked to solve
the riddle hidden
in the poem.

Questions that are answered to explain the
meaning of the poem.

Who, why, when, where?

What does it mean?
What does it seem?
What is it being?

NOTES

NOTES

NOTES